First World War
and Army of Occupation
War Diary
France, Belgium and Germany

18 DIVISION
Divisional Troops
C Squadron Westmorland and Cumberland Yeomanry
20 July 1915 - 30 April 1916

WO95/2024/1

The Naval & Military Press Ltd
www.nmarchive.com
Published in association with The National Archives

Published by

The Naval & Military Press Ltd

Unit 10 Ridgewood Industrial Park,
Uckfield, East Sussex,
TN22 5QE England
Tel: +44 (0) 1825 749494

www.naval-military-press.com

www.nmarchive.com

This diary has been reprinted in facsimile from the original. Any imperfections are inevitably reproduced and the quality may fall short of modern type and cartographic standards.

© **Crown Copyright**
Images reproduced by permission of The National Archives, London, England, 2015.

Contents

Document type	Place/Title	Date From	Date To
Heading	WO95/2024-1		
Heading	WO95/2024 (Part July 1917)		
Heading	WO95/2024 LSF/2/29 War Diary For B Battery 82nd Brigade 18th Division For July 1917		
Miscellaneous	WO95/2024 July 1917 missing		
Heading	18th Division 'C' Sqn West'd & Cum'd Yeo. Jly 1915-Apr 1916.To II Corps		
Heading	18th Division 'C' Division Westd & Cumbd Yeo Vol I And II July & August 15		
War Diary	Codford	20/07/1915	27/07/1915
War Diary	Havre	28/07/1915	28/07/1915
War Diary	Longeau	29/07/1915	29/07/1915
War Diary	Wargnies	29/07/1915	07/08/1915
War Diary	Frechencourt	09/08/1915	23/08/1915
War Diary	Ville-Sur-Ancre	24/08/1915	31/08/1915
Heading	18th Division 'C' Squadron Westd & Cumbd Yeomanry Vol 4 Oct 15		
War Diary	Ribemont	01/10/1915	31/10/1915
Heading	18th Division C Sq West & Cumb Yeo Vol 5 Nov 15		
War Diary	Ribemont	01/11/1915	30/11/1915
Heading	18th Div C Squadron West & Cumberland Yeo Vol 6 H.Q.		
War Diary	Ribemont	23/12/1915	31/12/1915
War Diary	Ribemont	12/12/1915	22/12/1915
War Diary	Ribemont	01/12/1915	11/12/1915
Heading	'C' St. West: Cumb Yeo. Vol 7		
War Diary	Ribemont	01/01/1916	31/01/1916
Heading	C St W & C Yeo Feb Vol 8		
War Diary	Ribemont	01/02/1916	02/02/1916
War Diary	Bonnay	03/02/1916	05/02/1916
War Diary	Pont Noyelles	06/02/1916	23/02/1916
War Diary	Bresle	24/02/1916	29/02/1916
Heading	C. Squad West & Cumb Yeo Vol 9		
War Diary	Bresle	01/03/1916	16/03/1916
War Diary	Chipilly	17/03/1916	30/04/1916

WP 95/2024 (1)
WP 95/2024 (1)

MISSING DOCUMENT

DO NOT PRODUCE

Document reference: WO 95/2024 (PART JULY 1917)

Date: 16/11/09

If found please pass to duty floor manager

(Floor managers to make available on DORIS and update APS electronic floor logs)

WO95/2024   LSF/2/29

War diary for
B Battery
82nd Brigade
18th Division

for July 1917

is missing

Jon Edgar
jaedgar@supanet.com

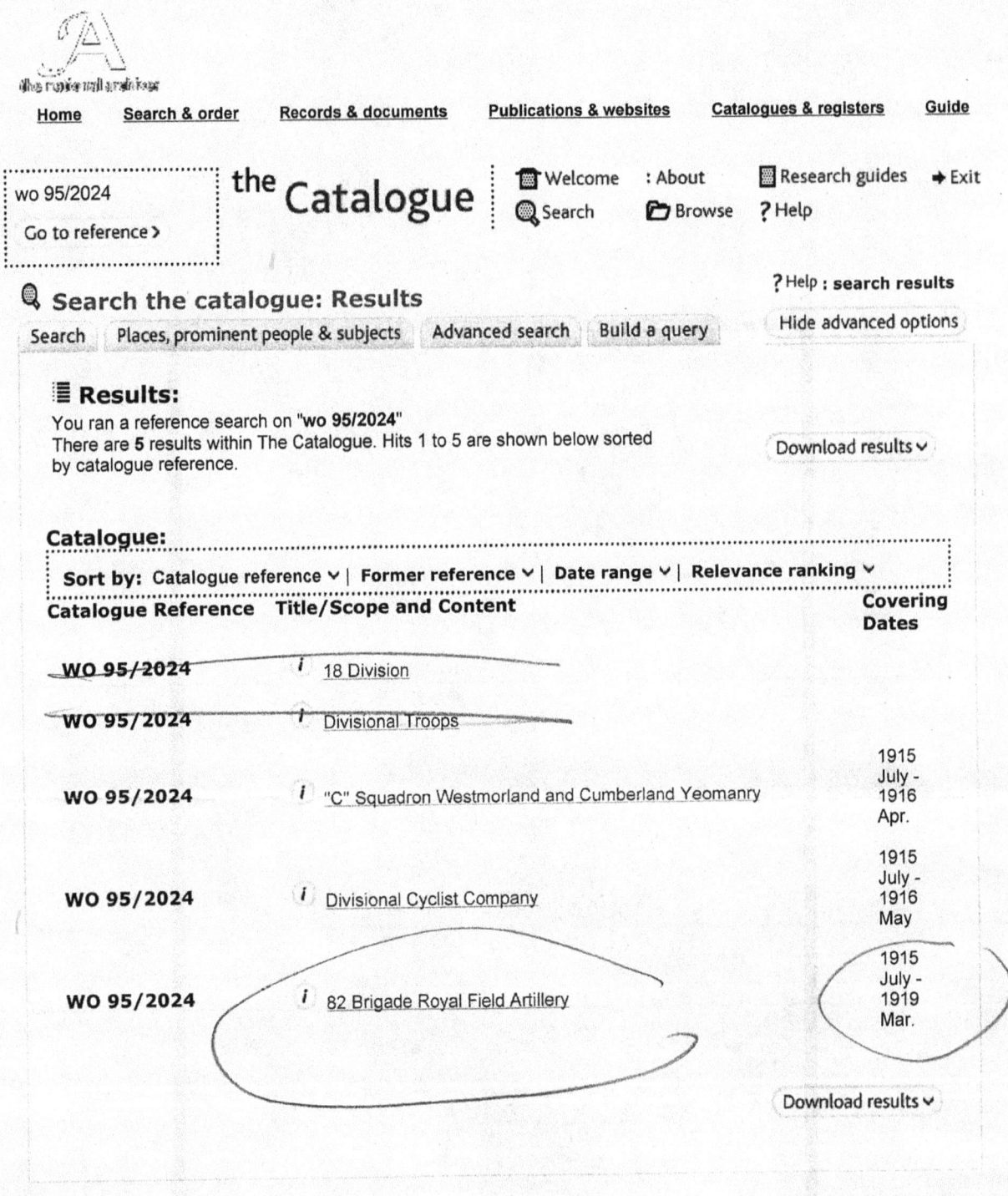

WO 95/2024
JULY 1917 missing

18TH DIVISION

'C' SQN WEST'D & CUM'D YEO.
JLY 1915-AUG 1916.

TO II CORPS

18th Hussain

$\frac{12}{7437}$

"C" Squadron West ? June & Yeo:
Vols I and II

July & August 15

April '16

WAR DIARY
or
INTELLIGENCE SUMMARY.

Army Form C. 2118.

Place	Date	Hour	Summary of Events and Information	Remarks and references to Appendices
CODFORD	20/7/15	-	Reduced to War Scale	C.W.V.
"	27/7/15	-	2 Troops entrained at WYLYE at 6.00 a.m.	
		8.15 a.m.	H.Q. and 2 Troops " " "	
			to SOUTHAMPTON DOCKS; embarked on S.S. ANGLO-CANADIAN and AFRICAN PRINCE respectively; sailed 4.30 p.m. and 6.30 p.m.	C.W.V.
HAVRE	29/7/15	10.0 a.m.	landed	
		10.15 p.m.	left GARE DES MARCHANDISES by train	
LONGEAU	29/7/15	8.00 a.m.	reached rail head and detrained; proceeded	C.W.V.
			March - route to FRESE WARGNIES arriving 3.15 p.m.; went into billets; attached South Infantry Bde. group.	
WARGNIES	"		Squadron Training	
	30/7/15	-	"	
	31/7/15	-	" ; Transferred 1 Sergt. 10 men to 18th Divisional H.Q. as G.O.C's escort.	C.W.V.
	1/8/15	-	Squadron Training	C.W.V.
	2/8/15	-	" ; parade for inspection by G.O.C. Xth Corps cancelled.	

Army Form C. 2118.

WAR DIARY
or
INTELLIGENCE SUMMARY.
(Erase heading not required.)

Instructions regarding War Diaries and Intelligence Summaries are contained in F. S. Regs., Part II. and the Staff Manual respectively. Title pages will be prepared in manuscript.

Place	Date	Hour	Summary of Events and Information	Remarks and references to Appendices
WARGNIES	2/8/15		Squadron Training	C.W.V.
"	3/8/15		"	C.W.V.
"	4/8/15		Inspection by G.O.C. Xth. Corps.	C.W.V.
"	5/8/15		Squadron Training	C.W.V.
"	6/8/15		" ; billeting party sent to new area in morn.	
"	7/8/15		postponed	C.W.V.
"	8/8/15		Proceeded by march route to FRECHENCOURT; billeted	C.W.V.
FRECHENCOURT	9/8/15		Squadron Training	C.W.V.
"	10/8/15		"	C.W.V.
"	11/8/15		"	C.W.V.
"	12/8/15		"	C.W.V.
"	13/8/15		"	C.W.V.
"	14/8/15		"	C.W.V.
"	15/8/15		Capt. D.C. BOLES 17th Lancers arrived to command 12th Divisional Mounted Troops; billeted with H.Q. Yeo.	C.W.V.
"	16/8/15		Squadron Training	C.W.V.

WAR DIARY
or
INTELLIGENCE SUMMARY.
(Erase heading not required.)

Army Form C. 2118.

Place	Date	Hour	Summary of Events and Information	Remarks and references to Appendices
FRECHENCOURT	17/8/15		Squadron Training	C.W.V.
"	18/8/15		"	C.W.V.
"	19/8/15		"	C.W.V.
"	20/8/15		"	C.W.V.
"	21/8/15		"	C.W.V.
"	22/8/15		Church Parade	C.W.V.
"	23/8/15	11.30a.m.	Proceeded by March Route to VILLE-SUR-ANCRE; billetted;	C.W.V.
VILLE-SUR-ANCRE	24/8/15		Squadron Training	C.W.V.
"	25/8/15		"	C.W.V.
"	26/8/15		" ; found 3 men as Traffic-control patrol + road to FRANVILLERS—HEILLY—AMIENS—ALBERT till further orders	C.W.V.
"	27/8/15		Squadron Training - very heavy rain at night	C.W.V.
"	28/8/15		"	C.W.V.
"	29/8/15		Church Parade	C.W.V.
"	30/8/15		Squadron Training	Weather conditions for month: fine and hot as a whole; very little rain	C.W.V.
"	31/8/15		"	C.W.V.

121/7432

18th Hussein

"C" Squadron Regt. Arab Yemen

Vol 4

Col 15

WAR DIARY
or
INTELLIGENCE SUMMARY.
(Erase heading not required.)

Army Form C. 2118.

Place	Date	Hour	Summary of Events and Information	Remarks and references to Appendices
BIBEMONT	1-10-15		Squadron Training	C.W.D.
"	2-10-15		" "	C.W.D.
"	3-10-15		Church Parade	C.W.D.
"	4-10-15		Squadron training	C.W.D.
"	5-10-15		" " in conjunction with M.M.G. on arrival of new M.G.	C.W.D.
"	6-10-15		Exercise; bath day	C.W.D.
"	7-10-15		" " Commenced getting horses undercover	C.W.V.
"	8-10-15		" " 2 Patrols found 6-8pm between Contal. Posts.	C.W.D.
"	9-10-15		Squadron training in conjunction with M.M.G. Batty	C.W.D.
"	10-10-15		Sunday	
"	11-10-15		Squadron training in conjunction with cyclists and M.M.G.	C.W.D.
"	12-10-15		Squadron Training. Capt Vans Lust Saddelin (4 other Ranks attachd)	
"	13-10-15	10	to 17 Lancers — Beautiful day.	W.M.G. hmg
"	13-10-15		Exercise Baths	hmg
"	14-10-15		Exercise - Baths - inspn of harness	W76

Army Form C. 2118.

WAR DIARY
or
INTELLIGENCE SUMMARY.
(Erase heading not required.)

Instructions regarding War Diaries and Intelligence Summaries are contained in F. S. Regs., Part II. and the Staff Manual respectively. Title pages will be prepared in manuscript.

Place	Date	Hour	Summary of Events and Information	Remarks and references to Appendices
Ribemont	15.10.15		Squadron Training	WTG
"	16.10.15		Farrier - afternoon musketry + Bayonet exercises.	WTG
"	17.10.15		Church Parade. Exercise.	WTG
"	18.10.15		Squadron Training —	WTG
"	19.10.15		Squadron Training in conjunction with Cyclists.	WTG
"	20.10.15		Baths. Exercise. Squadron football match v. horse guards	WTG
"	21.10.15		Baths. Night operations. Standing wt.	WTG
"	22.10.15		Squadron Training	WTG
"	23.10.15		Exercise	WTG
"	24.10.15		Church Parade. Exercise	WTG
"	25.10.15		First KINGS Inspection. a/t. Squadron Training	WTG
"	26.10.15		Squadron Training. 2nd Lt. Rhodes arrived.	WTG
"	27.10.15		Capt. Vane, Lieut. Gadsden & 4 O.R. returned to duty from 17th Lancers.	CWV
"	28.10.15		Baths.	CWV

WAR DIARY
or
INTELLIGENCE SUMMARY.

(Erase heading not required.)

Army Form C. 2118.

Place	Date	Hour	Summary of Events and Information	Remarks and references to Appendices
BIBEMONT	29-10-15		Squadron training in conjunction with Cyclist Coy	C.W.V
"	30-10-15		"	C.W.V.
"	31-10-15		Saddlery & arms inspection	C.W.V.
			Weather during month: fine and mild for first 3 weeks, thereafter wet and cold. All horses were got under cover about the middle of the month.	C.W.V.

C. W. Tow
Capt,
O.C. "C" Squadron
Westmorland & Cumberland Yeo.

18th Khurm / Col S: Mch: Quark: S20. vol. 5

121/7624

Nov 15

WAR DIARY
INTELLIGENCE SUMMARY

Army Form C. 2118.

Place	Date	Hour	Summary of Events and Information	Remarks and references to Appendices
RIBEMONT	1-11-15		Squadron Training, heavy rain; improving billets	C.W.J.
"	2-11-15		"	C.W.J.
"	3-11-15		Exercise	C.W.J.
"	4-11-15		Squadron training	C.W.J.
"	5-11-15		"	C.W.J.
"	6-11-15		"	C.W.J.
"	7-11-15		Church Parade; medical & billet inspection	C.W.J.
"	8-11-15		Exercise; Scout training; Bath day	C.W.J.
"	9		Scheme with Divisional Mounted Troops	W.R.
"	10		"	W.R.
"	11		Exercise; squadron training	W.R.
"	12		Squadron training	W.R.
"	13		Exercising	W.R.
"	14-11-15		Church Parade - Saddlery - B.W. inspection - Bath day	W.R.
"	15-11-15		Squadron Training	W.R.
"	16-11-15		Squadron Training	W.R.

Army Form C. 2118.

WAR DIARY
or
INTELLIGENCE SUMMARY.
(Erase heading not required.)

Instructions regarding War Diaries and Intelligence Summaries are contained in F. S. Regs., Part II. and the Staff Manual respectively. Title pages will be prepared in manuscript.

Place	Date	Hour	Summary of Events and Information	Remarks and references to Appendices
RIBEMONT	17-11-15		Squadron Training - B.W. hit trumpets	W.7
"	18-11-15		Exercise; improvements to billets	C.W.V.
"	19-11-15		Squadron training	C.W.V.
"	20-11-15		F service	C.W.V.
"	21-11-15		Church Parade; Saddlery and arms inspection	C.W.V.
"	22-11-15		Troop arrangements; improvements to billets	C.W.V.
"	23-11-15		"	C.W.V.
"	24-11-15		Squadron Training	C.W.V.
"	25-11-15		Exercise Capt W.H. Colwich went sick	C.W.V.
"			Took draft of 3 women on MERICOURT; no damage	C.W.V.
"	26-11-15		Squadron training; 3 Taubes bombed MERICOURT about 11 o'c; no structural damage to A.S.C. etc. a few casualties	C.W.V.
"	27-11-15		Exercise	C.W.V.
"	28-11-15		Church Parade; Saddlery and arms inspection	C.W.V.
"	29-11-15		Exercise; heavy rain	C.W.V.

Army Form C. 2118.

WAR DIARY
or
INTELLIGENCE SUMMARY.
(Erase heading not required.)

Place	Date	Hour	Summary of Events and Information	Remarks and references to Appendices
RIBEMONT	30-1-16		Exercise; Scouts Training	Cloudy
			Weather: Wet and cold for first 2 weeks; thereafter fine frosty; thaw set in from 25-1-16 tomorrow about 10 to 11 a.m.	

C. W. Lane
Capt.
Comdg "C" Sqdn
W.&T.d Wellington Horse
19th December
B.E.F.

Mr Sharon
with: Humboldt & Co.
Vol: 6

121/7935

18th [?]

J. Q.

Army Form C. 2118.

WAR DIARY
INTELLIGENCE SUMMARY.
(Erase heading not required.)

Instructions regarding War Diaries and Intelligence Summaries are contained in F.S. Regs., Part II. and the Staff Manual respectively. Title pages will be prepared in manuscript.

Place	Date	Hour	Summary of Events and Information	Remarks and references to Appendices
RIBEMONT	23-12-15		Squadron digging in telephone cable from GIBRALTAR to DERNANCOURT.	C.W.V.
"	24-12-15		Ditto	C.W.V.
"	25-12-15		30 men on coal fatigue at MERICOURT STATION	C.W.V.
"	26-12-15		Church Parade. Saddlery + ammunition	C.W.V.
"	27-12-15		Squadron digging in telephone cable each 23-24/12/15	C.W.V.
"	28-12-15		Riding School for horse stampings	C.W.V.
"	29-12-15		Making horse stampings	C.W.V.
"	30-12-15		"	C.W.V.
"	31-12-15		Fatigues at coal yard and R.F. Park at AILBEMONT/ SUGAENE	C.W.V.
			Weather conditions for month: Very mild, mild as a whole; rain fall considerable	

C.W. Tong Capt.
O/C. C Sqdn. Warwickshire Yeo.

WAR DIARY
or
INTELLIGENCE SUMMARY.
(Erase heading not required.)

Army Form C. 2118.

Place	Date	Hour	Summary of Events and Information	Remarks and references to Appendices
RIBEMONT	12-12-15		Church Parade. 2/Lt. C.F. Taylor and 8 men arrived as reinforcements.	C.W.V.
"	13-12-15		Squadron training.	C.W.V.
"			11th Troop (Lieut Guthrie) 11th Troop commenced with digging Machine gun emplacement at BECORDEL	
"	14-12-15		Exercise. 1st Troop digging at BECORDEL	C.W.V.
"	15-12-15		2nd Troop (2/Lt. Fay) day digging at BECORDEL.	C.W.V.
			B.B.	C.W.V.
"	16-12-15		Found Patrols &c of Divisional Area	C.W.V.
"	17-12-15		"	C.W.V.
"	18-12-15		Exercise. 2nd. Troop digging at BECORDEL at night	C.W.V.
"	19-12-15		Church Parade	C.W.V.
"	20-12-15		Officers reconnaissance of country from DERNANCOURT to GIBRALTAR.	C.W.V.
"	21-12-15		Squadron reconnaissance as above	C.W.V.
"	22-12-15		"	C.W.V.

WAR DIARY
or
INTELLIGENCE SUMMARY.
(Erase heading not required.)

Army Form C. 2118.

Instructions regarding War Diaries and Intelligence Summaries are contained in F. S. Regs., Part II. and the Staff Manual respectively. Title pages will be prepared in manuscript.

Place	Date	Hour	Summary of Events and Information	Remarks and references to Appendices
RIBEMONT	1-12-15		Squadron Training	C.W.V.
"	2-12-15		Exercise	C.W.V.
"	3-12-15		Squadron Training; heavy rain	C.W.V.
"	4-12-15		Exercise	C.W.V.
"	5-12-15		Church Parade at MERICOURT and inspection by G.O.C. 12th Divn	C.W.V.
"	6-12-15		Squadron Training	C.W.V.
"	7-12-15		Exercise	C.W.V.
"	8-12-15		Squadron Training; 3rd Troop (Lt. Roberts) digging machine gun emplacement at BECORDEL at night	C.W.V.
"	9-12-15		Exercise; 1st Troop (Lt. Rhodes) digging machine gun emplacement at BECORDEL at night & lay tram alley	C.W.V.
"	10-12-15		Exercise	C.W.V.
"	11-12-15		; operations in neighbourhood of BOUZINCOURT, MILLENCOURT and ROUTE NATIONALE No 29 men at rest in connection with suppose d signalling enemy at A BOISSELLE; operations started 11/. m. C.W.V. no results.	C.W.V.

"C" Af: Woch: Rund: Yes:
Vol. 7

Army Form C. 2118.

WAR DIARY
INTELLIGENCE SUMMARY.
(Erase heading not required.)

Instructions regarding War Diaries and Intelligence Summaries are contained in F.S. Regs., Part II. and the Staff Manual respectively. Title pages will be prepared in manuscript.

Place	Date	Hour	Summary of Events and Information	Remarks and references to Appendices
RIBEMONT	1-1-16		Making standings	C.W.J.
"	2-1-16		Special Church Parade at MERICOURT. 3rd Troop (2/Lt. Roberts) digging M.G. emplacement on CRAWLEY RIDGE at night	C.W.J.
"	3-1-16		Examination of signallers; making standings; coalyard fatigue 15 men.	C.W.J.
"	4-1-16		Bath day; making standings.	C.W.J.
"	5-1-16		" " squadron digging	C.W.J.
"	6-11½am		communication trench for M.G. west of PERTH AVENUE	C.W.J.
"	6-1-16		Bath day; loading bricks for standing	C.W.J.
"	7-1-16		Squadron digging as 6-1-16 6 to 2 pm — 11 a.m.	C.W.J.
"	8-1-16		Coal fatigue at railhead.	C.W.J.
"	9-1-16		Church Parade; saddlery & arms inspection	C.W.J.
"	10-1-16		Coal fatigue; horses inspected with mallein	C.W.J.
"	11-1-16		"	C.W.J.
"	12-1-16		Squadron digging as on 7-1-16. Reveille (slight)	C.W.J.
"	13-1-16		Exercise; Brush & Signal	C.W.J.

Army Form C. 2118.

WAR DIARY
or
INTELLIGENCE SUMMARY.
(Erase heading not required.)

Instructions regarding War Diaries and Intelligence Summaries are contained in F.S. Regs., Part II. and the Staff Manual respectively. Title pages will be prepared in manuscript.

Place	Date	Hour	Summary of Events and Information	Remarks and references to Appendices
RIBEMONT	14-1-16		Squadron digging as on 12-1-16	C.W.J.
"	15-1-16		Exercise; g'pay	C.W.J.
"	16-1-16		Church Parade; saddlery & arms inspection	C.W.J.
"	17-1-16		Squadron digging as on 12-1-16 { 2/Lt. A.H. Parker	C.W.J.
"	18-1-16		" reported for duty	C.W.J.
"	18-1-16		Exercise	C.W.J.
"	19-1-16		Squadron training; draft stable-riding	C.W.J.
"	20-1-16		"	C.W.J.
"	21-1-16		Bath day	C.W.J.
"	22-1-16		Fatigue for D.S.C.	C.W.J.
"	23-1-16		"	C.W.J.
"	24-1-16		" Church Parade	C.W.J.
"	25-1-16		"	C.W.J.
"	26-1-16		"	C.W.J.
"	26-1-16		Reconnaissance of neighbourhood of ALBERT and BECADEL for communication purposes	C.W.J.
"	27-1-16		Fatigue for D.S.C.	C.W.J.

Army Form C. 2118.

WAR DIARY
INTELLIGENCE SUMMARY.
(Erase heading not required.)

Instructions regarding War Diaries and Intelligence Summaries are contained in F. S. Regs., Part II. and the Staff Manual respectively. Title pages will be prepared in manuscript.

Place	Date	Hour	Summary of Events and Information	Remarks and references to Appendices
BIBEMONT	28-1-16		Dismounted parade; Sergt. Roberts to D.H.Q. vice Sgt. Taylor to duty	C.W.V.
"	29-1-16		Bath day	C.W.V.
"	30-1-16		Church Parade; saddlery & arms inspection	C.W.V.
"	31-1-16		Exercise	C.W.V.

Weather abnormally mild; not very much rain

C.W. Lane Capt.
O.C. (C) Sqdn.
1/1 Westd. Ymn. Cavalry Yeo.

Cn Sqd. W+C. Yeo

R   Feb
       Vol 8

Army Form C. 2118.

WAR DIARY
or
INTELLIGENCE SUMMARY.
(Erase heading not required.)

Instructions regarding War Diaries and Intelligence Summaries are contained in F. S. Regs., Part II. and the Staff Manual respectively. Title pages will be prepared in manuscript.

Place	Date	Hour	Summary of Events and Information	Remarks and references to Appendices
RIBEMONT	1-2-16		Preparations for move	C.W.V.
"	2-2-16		Proceeded by march - route to BONNAY; move recounciled owing to alteration in divisional order	C.W.V.
BONNAY	3-2-16		Exercise	C.W.V.
"	4-2-16		"	C.W.V.
"	5-2-16		Proceeded by march - route to PONT NOYELLES	C.W.V.
PONT NOYELLES	6-2-16		Settling into billets; 1st Troop, 3rd Troop detached to horse training in open reconnaissance under cover	C.W.V.
"	7-2-16		Squadron training	C.W.V.
"	8-2-16		"	C.W.V.
"	9-2-16		"	C.W.V.
"	10-2-16		"	P.W.V.
"	11-2-16		Very heavy rain	C.W.V.
"	12-2-16		Exercise	C.W.V.
"	13-2-16		Church Parade	C.W.V.
"	14-2-16		Squadron training	C.W.V.
"	15-2-16		Recruits training. 1 Sergt. w.g.o.R. to A.P.M. 18th Division for instruction in Police duties	C.W.V.

WAR DIARY

INTELLIGENCE SUMMARY.

(Erase heading not required.)

Army Form C. 2118.

Instructions regarding War Diaries and Intelligence Summaries are contained in F.S. Regs, Part II. and the Staff Manual respectively. Title pages will be prepared in manuscript.

Place	Date	Hour	Summary of Events and Information	Remarks and references to Appendices
PONT NOYELLES	16/2/16		Heavy rain; exercise	C.W.V.
"	17/2/16		Bath day	C.W.V.
"	18/2/16		Exercise; heavy rain	C.W.V.
"	19/2/16		" "	C.W.V.
"	20/2/16		Church Parade	C.W.V.
"	21/2/16		Bath day; Squadron Training, 1 Sqdn.	C.W.V.
"	22/2/16		Squadron Training; some work	C.W.V.
"	23/2/16		Proceeded by march route to BRESLE; forenoon storm afternoon	C.W.V.
BRESLE	24/2/16		Exercise; hard frost	C.W.V.
"	25/2/16		1 Sergt. to O.R. to A.P.M. 18th Division for instruction in Police duties. 1 Sergt. + 9 O.R. to duty from A.P.M. 18 O.R. – D amunition Training	C.W.V.
"	26/2/16		Squadron training, dismounted; thaw	C.W.V.
"	27/2/16		Church Parade; thaw	C.W.V.
"	28/2/16		Thaw; Squadron Training; Sergt + 9 O.R. to A.P.M. 18th Division for one week instruction in Police duty	C.W.V.

WAR DIARY
INTELLIGENCE SUMMARY

Army Form C. 2118.

Place	Date	Hour	Summary of Events and Information	Remarks and references to Appendices
BRESLE	29/2/18		Écurie	C.o.2.
			Weather: cold throughout; very wet joints 3 weeks; snow a frost continued	

C. W. Lane Capt.
O.C. "C" Sqdn
1/1 Westmorland & Cumberland Yeo.
18th Divn.

C. Savin
were to come to
Vol 9

WAR DIARY

INTELLIGENCE SUMMARY

Army Form C. 2118.

(Erase heading not required.)

Instructions regarding War Diaries and Intelligence Summaries are contained in F.S. Regs., Part II. and the Staff Manual respectively. Title pages will be prepared in manuscript.

Place	Date	Hour	Summary of Events and Information	Remarks and references to Appendices
BRESLE	1-3-16		Squadron training	O.W.V.
"	2-3-16		"	O.W.V.
"	3-3-16		Exercise	O.W.V.
"	4-3-16		"	O.W.V.
"	5-3-16		Saddlery & Arms Inspection	O.W.V.
"	6-3-16		Squadron training	O.W.V.
"	7-3-16		"	O.W.V.
"	8-3-16		Tactical Exercise	O.W.V.
"	9-3-16		Squadron training	O.W.V.
"	10-3-16		"	O.W.V.
"	11-3-16		Exercise	O.W.V.
"	12-3-16		Saddlery & Arms Inspection	O.W.V.
"	13-3-16		Troop Training	O.W.V.
"	14-3-16		Exercise: Advance Party to CHIPILLY	O.W.V.
"	15-3-16		Moved by road to CHIPILLY	O.W.V.
"	16-3-16		Settling in to billets, exercise	O.W.V.

WAR DIARY
INTELLIGENCE SUMMARY.
(Erase heading not required.)

Army Form C. 2118.

Place	Date	Hour	Summary of Events and Information	Remarks and references to Appendices
CHIPILLY	17-3-16		Exercise	
"	18-3-16		Took over Block-ade Posts at CHIPILLY (5 posts) SAILLY LORETTE, MEAULTE at Lock & CAPPY BRIDGE - in all 13 N.C.O.s & men. Found 6 men for M.P.	
"	19-3-16		Exercise	
"	20-3-16		Reconnaissance of country E of BRAY for leave purposes	C in W &
"	21-3-16		ditto	C in W &
"	22-3-16		ditto	C in W &
"	23-3-16		ditto	C in W &
"	24-3-16		Exercise, movement	C in W &
"	25-3-16		Reconnaissance of country E of BRAY for leave purposes	C in W &
"	26-3-16		Exercise	C in W &
"	27-3-16		ditto as on 25-3-16	C in W &
"	28-3-16		ditto	C in W &

Army Form C. 2118.

WAR DIARY
— or —
INTELLIGENCE SUMMARY.
(Erase heading not required.)

Instructions regarding War Diaries and Intelligence Summaries are contained in F. S. Regs., Part II. and the Staff Manual respectively. Title pages will be prepared in manuscript.

Place	Date	Hour	Summary of Events and Information	Remarks and references to Appendices
CHIPILLY	29-3-16		Reconnaissance of country E. of BRAY for raiding purposes.	
"	30-3-16		Ditto	
"	31-3-16		Ditto.	
			Weather: snow first week, followed by very mild firm weather for a week, then cold, some sleet and snow, country drying up rapidly.	

C. W. Ley
Capt.
O.C. (C) Sqdn 1st advance Hqrs.
1/1 West Somerset Yeo.
18th Division.

C Sqd 1st W + CY

WAR DIARY

INTELLIGENCE SUMMARY.
(Erase heading not required.)

Army Form C. 2118.

Place	Date	Hour	Summary of Events and Information	Remarks and references to Appendices
CHIPILLY	1-4-16		Billets etc inspected by Divisional Commander	Cww
"	2-4-16		2/Lt Taylor, 1 N.C.O & 2 O.R attached 54th INF BDE for liaison duties.	Cww
"	3-4-16		Reconnaissance for bivouac purposes	Cww
"	4-4-16		" " " " Lt Rhodes	
"			1 N.C.O & 2 O.R attached 55th INF BDE for liaison duties	Cww
"	5-4-16		Reconnaissance for bivouac purposes	Cww
"	6-4-16		Ditto	
"	7-4-16		Ditto 2/Lt Taylor, 1 N.C.O & 2 O.R to bring post 54th INF BDE.	Cww
"	8-4-16		Lt Rhodes, 1 N.C.O & 2 O.R on liaison duty from 55th INF BDE	Cww
"	9-4-16		Inspection of arms, saddlery, billets etc	Cww
"	10-4-16		Practice of liaison duties	Cww
"	11-4-16		Exercise	Cww
"	12-4-16		Practice of liaison duties	Cww

WAR DIARY
INTELLIGENCE SUMMARY
(Erase heading not required.)

Army Form C. 2118.

Instructions regarding War Diaries and Intelligence Summaries are contained in F. S. Regs., Part II. and the Staff Manual respectively. Title pages will be prepared in manuscript.

Place	Date	Hour	Summary of Events and Information	Remarks and references to Appendices
CHIPILLY	13-4-16		Practice of liaison duties	C.W.J.
"	14-4-16		Ditto	C.W.J.
"	15-4-16		Ditto	C.W.J.
"	16-4-16		Billet inspection	C.W.J.
"	17-4-16		Practice of liaison duties	C.W.J.
"	18-4-16		Heavy rain, scarcely no	C.W.J.
"	19-4-16		Practice of liaison duties at night	C.W.J.
"	20-4-16		Exercise	C.W.J.
"	21-4-16		Practice of liaison duties	C.W.J.
"	22-4-16		Ditto	C.W.J.
"	23-4-16		Billet inspection	C.W.J.
"	24-4-16		Practice of liaison duties	C.W.J.
"	25-4-16		Ditto at night	C.W.J.
"	26-4-16		Exercise	C.W.J.
"	27-4-16		Practice of liaison duties	C.W.J.
"	28-4-16		Ditto	C.W.J.

WAR DIARY
INTELLIGENCE SUMMARY
(Erase heading not required.)

Army Form C. 2118.

Place	Date	Hour	Summary of Events and Information	Remarks and references to Appendices
Chilly	29/4/16		Horse inspection. Practice of Linen Screen. Exercise. Repairs Billets, during tonight.	WZ 1074
"	30/4/16		Windier. Cold and wet in the early part of the day but warmer and settled during the latter part of the day.	

W. Haddow Capt.
for O.C. "C" Sqdn.
1/1 Westmoreland & Cumberland Yeomanry

www.ingramcontent.com/pod-product-compliance
Lightning Source LLC
Chambersburg PA
CBHW081500160426
43193CB00013B/2542